Baseball's Best Sluggers

By
Bob Hunter

School Book Fairs, Inc.
Columbus, Ohio

Bob Hunter is a sportswriter in Columbus, Ohio.

Cover Photo: Courtesy of the Philadelphia Phillies.

Inside Photos: Courtesy
Philadelphia Phillies, pages 21, 73
Los Angeles Dodgers, pages 26, 31
St. Louis Cardinals, page 51
Boston Red Sox, pages 84, 88, 123, 126
New York Yankees, pages 96, 102
Minnesota Twins, page 112
United Press International, pages 15, 40, 46, 61, 76

Copyright © 1979 By School Book Fairs, Inc.

Table of Contents

Pete Rose 7
Steve Garvey 23
Dave Parker 34
Lou Brock 44
Johnny Bench 54
Mike Schmidt 68
Jim Rice 80
Reggie Jackson 91
Rod Carew 107
Carl Yastrzemski 118

Baseball's Best Sluggers

Pete Rose

Week after week fans watched for Pete Rose to pass the 3,000-hit mark. He finally made it on May 5, 1978. His 3,000 hits should have been the final achievement in a grand career. But less than two months later, Rose was making headlines again.

He went on a hitting streak that sent him after the record for hitting in consecutive games. No man in the history of baseball over 30 years old had ever hit in 30 games in a row. "If I break it, then go and win the National League batting title, maybe you guys will stop telling me how old I am," Rose told reporters.

He broke the 30 mark. Then he broke Tommy Holmes modern NL record of 37. Then he went after Joe DiMaggio's supposedly unbreakable all-time mark of 56 games. He didn't break it. His hitting streak snapped at 44 games. He tied Willie Keeler's 1897 record for the second longest streak in baseball history.

The day after his streak ended, he collected four hits. That appeared to be punishment for the Atlanta Brave pitching staff who had stopped his streak. But Rose wouldn't get involved with such ideas. "I didn't try any harder than I did last night," said Rose, explaining his four-hit effort. "I think I have a chance to win the batting title. And you have to accumulate the hits and add them up."

Few men are still playing baseball at 37. But Rose is not one of the crowd. He has been apart from the others from the day he signed his first professional baseball contract. He has stayed that way ever since. More than anyone in the game, Rose marches to the beat of a different drummer.

That wasn't always a plus. When Rose came up, the veterans on the Reds resented the way the rookie second baseman ran to first after walks. They resented his display of "hustle". He was a "hot dog" in their minds. Thus, the native Cincinnatian had a difficult time at first. But Rose wasn't about to change his style of play. It was what gave him a shot at the big leagues in the first place. It was what will eventually earn him a spot in the Hall of Fame. It's the Pete Rose style. That's why they call him "Charlie Hustle".

Little Pete grew up in an athletic family. His father, Pete Sr., once served as a sparring partner for former world featherweight boxing champion Freddie Miller. His father also played football in the rugged Cincinnati semi-professional leagues until he was well over 40. No wonder his father gave Pete his first pair of boxing gloves when he was only one year old. He gave his son his first baseball glove not long after that. As soon as he was eligible, Rose joined the local youth baseball and football leagues. When he was nine, his father taught him to be a switch-hitter.

"My father worked hard with me," said Rose. "But he was worried that a coach of a knothole team might not like the idea and not let me switch-hit. So my dad went to the coach and said 'Look, I want you to promise me one thing. No matter what the situation, game-winning run on third base or anything, I want Pete to be able to switch-hit.' The coach agreed and that's how I became a switch-hitter—that and a lot of hard work, especially left-handed."

Pete also learned the habit of running to first on base-on-balls. One day, he was watching a baseball game on television with his father. He saw Enos Slaughter, then a star outfielder with the St. Louis Cardinals, run to first base following a walk.

"My father turned to me and said, 'There, that's the way baseball ought to be played,' " said Rose. "And the idea stuck with me."

Rose had to play hard. Today Rose stands 5'11" and weighs a solid 200 pounds. But he was a scrawny 5'7", 145-pounder when he signed to play with the Reds back in 1960. He might not have been signed at all but his uncle was a scout in the Reds' system. Rose wasn't a great prospect. He had to hustle for everything he could get. As Rose said after his 3,000th career hit. "Nobody has given me a thing. I couldn't become the best home run hitter or the best RBI man, but I worked hours and hours on the nature of my game, which is switch-hitting. The whole secret is not trying to be something you're not."

During his first summer in pro ball Rose hit .277 for Geneva of the New York-Pennsylvania League. Then he was promoted to the Reds' Tampa farm club in the Florida State League in 1961. He first showed signs of becoming a great hitter there. He hit .331. He had 20 doubles, 30 triples and a league-leading 160 hits. In 1962 Rose moved on to

Macon in the Sally League. He hit .330.

The fans around that circuit began to call him "Hollywood" because of his hustling tendencies. Cincinnati Manager Fred Hutchinson was impressed. Rose had grown into a 5'11", 190-pound mass of energy. He became one of the Reds' best prospects. To the veterans' dismay, he made the big club the following spring.

"It was a team of cliques," said Rose, recalling how the players hung around in groups and rejected outsiders. "Me, I was the brash kid. They rejected me. I was on Cloud Nine and didn't even realize it."

"A writer took a poll at the Causeway Inn, where we stayed—yes or no, did the players think that Pete Rose was gonna make it. Out of 17 guys, only one said yes...Don Blasingame."

Blasingame was the guy who Rose would replace at second base. Reds' Manager Fred Hutchinson started Rose there on opening day. In his first 23 trips to the plate, Pete got only three hits. He was soon benched. The Cincinnati manager understood that Rose was nervous. He gave him a chance to get settled. Then he put him in the lineup against the Astros on April 27, 1963. Rose remained in the Reds' lineup for the next 15 years.

That season the Cincinnati second baseman hit .273. He earned the National League's Rookie of the Year award. He followed up with another good, but unspectacular, year in 1964. He hit .269. In 1965 he played in all 162 games and hit .312. With his first 200-hit season, Pete Rose was on his way.

Others on the club complained that Cincinnati was a poor place to play because they couldn't make as much money as a player in New York or Chicago. But Rose disagreed. He predicted that he was going to become the first $100,000 singles' hitter in the game. He piled one .300 season on another throughout the 1960's.

He hit .313 in 1966 and .301 in 1967. In 1968 he proved himself to be the clutch player. Rose had an outstanding year at the plate. He outpolled all other players for a starting spot in the All-Star game. Then he missed it because of a broken thumb. He battled Pittsburgh's Matty Alou down to the wire for the National League batting championship. The two were almost tied going into the final two days. Then Rose disposed of Alou with a 5-for-5 day on the next to the last day of the season. He clinched it on the final day of the season with a 1-for-3 effort. Alou went hitless. Rose's final average was .355 to win the NL batting title. And he had another 200-hit season (210) in spite of missing three weeks of play because of the thumb injury.

"Pete is the most pressure proof person I have ever known," said his wife, Karolyn, during Rose's 44-game hitting streak. "The things that might drive you and I right up the wall, they don't bother Pete a bit. In fact, I think they're a stimulant."

"Pressure is Pete's second cup of coffee in the morning. It's what gets him going, keeps him going. He really thrives on it.

The more there is, the better he plays," she added.

He proved that when he repeated his batting feat in 1969. With two weeks remaining in the season, Pete trailed league leader Cleon Jones of the New York Mets by eight points. This time he edged out Pittsburgh's Roberto Clemente on the last day of the season. 1969 was the fifth straight season that Rose had hit over .300.

In 1970 manager Sparky Anderson had made Rose Team captain. He deserved the role. Every member of the club looked on him as a leader.

Pete was also the most consistent Red's hitter throughout the 1970's. He managed to stay above the .300 mark and above or near the 200-hit mark every season but 1974. And his 1974 statistics— .284 average with a league-leading total in doubles (45) and runs scored (51)—weren't that bad for the average ballplayer. The problem, of course, is that Rose isn't average.

In 1973, Rose hit .338, knocked 230 hits, and won the third batting title. He led the team into the playoffs against the surprising New York Mets. Rose had always been a target of the New York boo birds. In the third game of the Series he slid into second base. He got up and got into a shoving match with New York shortstop Bud Harrelson. When Rose returned to left field, he was showered with bottles, garbage and all sorts of litter. Anderson saw the crowd throwing things at Rose. He pulled his team off the field. The Reds lost 9-2. Rose's fight made the entire Shea Stadium crowd his enemies.

He got revenge in the fourth game. A New York fan gave him a beer shower. Then Rose silenced the boo birds with a 12th inning homer. The homer lifted the Reds to a 2-1 victory. He circled the bases with his fist clinched high in the air. Unfortunately for Rose and the Reds, however, the Mets won the pennant with a 7-2 victory in game five.

He was able to do a mini-repeat of the New York scene a couple of months later. The president of the Baseball Writers Association called him with the news that he had been named the National League's Most Valuable Player. "I clinched my fist and waved it in the air," he recalled. It was a symbol he would use again and again. He used it whenever he reached another milestone.

There are many. Rose's list of records and accomplishments is remarkable. At the age of 37 he's still adding to his totals. He has more hits than any other switch-hitter. He has been a National League All-Star at three positions, second base, outfield and third base. He seems certain to break Ty Cobb's record of nine 200-hit seasons in 1979, when he goes for his tenth. There seems to be no end to his achievements.

"Pete is one of the greatest players of all time," said Cincinnati Manager Sparky Anderson. "About the only way to describe the guy is to say he is amazing."

"No one gets more out of his God-given talent than Rose. No player is more durable. You have to fight him to keep him out of the lineup, even when you know that he's hurting."

When Rose played on opening day, 1978, he broke Cincinnati's all-time record for consecutive games played (652). He continued to play throughout the early season until an illness forced him to sit out the second game of a double-header.

Seeing that string snapped didn't bother Pete. He had more important things to do including another National League West title. The part he played in winning the two World Series rings he won may be his proudest accomplishment of all. He doesn't make any bones about the fact that he'd like to win a couple of more before he's through.

"My top goal now is winning a division championship and getting into the World Series again," said Rose, after singling off Montreal's Steve Rogers for his 3,000th major league hit. "This was a big hit, but the biggest hit I ever got was the one that tied the seventh game of the (1975) World Series against Boston because that gave Joe Morgan a chance to win it." It is the kind of team thinking that has made Rose the valuable player that he is. What goals are left for Rose to pursue? He would like to pass Stan Musial's mark of 3,630 hits and become the all-time National League leader in lifetime hits.

"I don't think getting Ty Cobb's record (4,191) is possible," said Rose. "But 3,631 is. That would top Musial's all-time National League record and I'd like that."

The way Rose was tearing through the league in 1978, it doesn't look like he has too much to worry about. In fact, Rose gave the public a tip-off to his determination immediately after he had lined Rogers' fastball for his 3,000th career hit.

Expo first baseman Tony Perez retrieved the 3,000th hit ball. He handed it to Rose at first.

What did Rose say as 37,823 fans roared their approval? Perez laughs when he recalls the moment. "The first thing he said to me," said Perez, "was 'I get two more times at bat. That means I can still get two more hits.' " It was a typical Rose reaction.

At the end of the 1978 season, Rose and the Reds' management couldn't

agree on a new contract. Rose became a free agent. Many people were saying that Rose should stay in Cincinnati. Manager Sparky Anderson said, "Pete Rose is the Cincinnati Reds". Shortly after the free agent draft, Anderson was fired by the Reds, and John McNamara was their new manager. A few weeks later, Rose signed a contract to play for the Philadelphia Phillies. As their leading switch hitter in baseball history, Rose was finally leaving his home town of Cincinnati.

The Phillies had lost three straight years in the playoffs. But, Rose felt that all the Phillies lacked was a team leader and a good leadoff hitter. Paul Owens, the Phils' director of player personnel, was excited. Owens explained what Rose meant to the Phillies. "He's proud. He works hard. He's a team leader. By himself, Rose couldn't turn a club around but with a contending team, he could be the difference between a winner and a bridesmaid."

Is Pete Rose a winner? You bet he is!

Steve Garvey

As a young boy Steve Garvey dreamed of playing for the Dodgers. His childhood idol was Gil Hodges. Hodges was the Dodgers' first baseman. "Gil Hodges was my hero, on and off the field," Garvey recalls. "He was a perfect gentleman at all times. His handshake was something I still remember." Steve wanted to follow in his footsteps. Unlike most young boys, Steve's dream did come true. Today, Steve Garvey IS the spirit of the Dodgers. Now, he is the first baseman. He is also one of the league's most-feared hitters.

"I sincerely believe that there is such a

thing as a Dodger," Garvey said. "I don't think there's such a thing as a Padre or a Brave or a Met. I sincerely think that I was born to be a Dodger."

Steven Patrick Garvey was born in Tampa, Florida on December 22, 1948. His father, Joe, was a Greyhound bus driver. Joe drove the Dodgers' team bus when the club trained in Florida. Sometimes Steve would go along. He would be a batboy.

As a kid, he practiced hitting grapefruits. The Garveys had 11 grapefruit trees in their yard. So there were many "balls" for young Steve to hit. He says, "In the spring I'd take the little hard grapefruits that had fallen off and I'd hit them with a broomstick. I'd be the whole Dodger lineup, Charlie Neal, Gilliam, Campanella, Snider, Hodges. As a grapefruit hitter I was a line drive hitter, even then it must have been my build."

Steve played Little League. He hit .750 with 18 home runs in 20 games. In his first four innings in Pony League ball, he hit for the cycle. That means he hit a single, a double, a triple and a home run. "Little things like that happened to me along the line," he says, "that made me think, 'Maybe I am destined to be a professional athlete.'"

In high school Garvey starred in baseball. He also played quarterback on the football team. His senior year he gained more than 1,000 yards both running and passing.

He went to college at Michigan State. He played defensive back. He was a starter in his sophomore year. But in 1968 he was drafted by the Dodgers. He left school to join the team.

His first year he played in the Ogden, Utah Pioneer League. His batting average was .338 with 20 homers and 59 RBIs. The following year he played in Albuquerque in the Class AA Texas league. His average jumped to .373 with 14 home runs. In 1970 Garvey played three games with the Dodgers. But he got off to a slow start. He was sent to Spokane. He played in the Triple-A Pacific League the rest of the season.

In 1971 Steve Garvey made it to the majors. He played 81 games and hit .227 with seven home runs. He played third base. That year he was best known for his throwing errors. He had separated his shoulder in college football. His arm just wasn't strong enough for long throws.

After the 1971 season, Steve Garvey

got married. He and his wife, Cyndy, spent the winter in the Dominican Republic. The Dodgers sent Steve there to play ball. They hoped it would strengthen his arm.

When he returned to the Dodgers in 1972, he was still a substitute player. He hit .269 in 96 games with nine homers and 30 RBIs.

By 1973, the Dodgers' Manager Walt Alston was beginning to wonder what to do with Steve Garvey. Alston decided to try him in left field. Steve only lasted there a couple of weeks. He was benched. He didn't start a game for two months. He was only used as a pinch hitter. Then Alston gave Garvey a chance to start at first base. That season his batting average jumped to .304.

Steve Garvey's dream finally came true in 1974. Garvey got into the regular line-up as first baseman. Since he only played 76 games in 1973, he was not on the All-Star Ballot in 1974. But thanks to a million write-in votes, he made the All-Star team. Only one other player had ever made the starting lineup for an All-Star game by write-in vote. That was Rico Carty in 1970. Once in the game, Garvey collected two hits. He also made two outstanding plays in the field. He was voted Most Valuable Player. Steve went on to bat .312 and hit 21 homers that season. He also batted in 111 runs.

Thanks to Garvey's help, Los Angeles won the NL West. The team went on to win the pennant. They beat the Pittsburgh Pirates in four games. Garvey had a .389 average in the championship series. In the World Series. Garvey was the Dodgers' leading hitter. But Los Angeles lost to the Oakland Athletics in five games.

Steve Garvey had made it. He received the Golden Glove Award as the league's best fielding first baseman. He was also named the National League's Most Valuable Player. "Any success I have had is directly or indirectly due to the other players on the team," Garvey said. "This could not have been possible without the other players. The whole season is a culmination of Walter Alston's confidence in me. And the key to my success is my wife."

Cyndy helped make the year successful in another way. While Steve was playing in the World Series, she had a baby. The baby girl, Krisha Lee, was born on October 16, 1974.

After the 1974 season, Steve Garvey received lots of publicity. Some people called him the "all-American boy". Others called him a "goody-goody". He said, "I am what I am. What I do is what I really want to do. I am genuinely interested in doing all I can for baseball and for people who are less fortunate. I believe in helping children, I believe in being a good Catholic, and I believe in treating other people like I would like to be treated. If that's a goody-goody person, I guess I am one."

Garvey spends a great deal of time visiting children's hospitals and speaking to youth groups. One of his favorite stories is about a boy named Ricky Williams. Steve visited Ricky in the hospital in 1971. Ricky had just had part of his lower leg cut off. The 10-year old had cancer. The doctors said he had an 18 percent chance of living. Garvey tells the rest. "I don't really believe that I have any special powers. But Ricky that night gave me a medal, with an inscription that said, 'To Steve Garvey. Thank you for giving me the will to live.'" In 1974 Ricky Williams walked with Steve Garvey from the dugout to first base. It was the annual night for crippled children.

The next year, 1975, was another good one for the 5'10", 190-pounder. Garvey batted .319. He had 210 hits, 95 RBIs and 18 homers. But the Dodgers finished in second place. They ended the season 20 games behind the Cincinnati Reds.

In 1976, Garvey hit .317. He knocked 200 hits, batted in 80 runs and hit 13 home runs. He played in all 162 games that season. Again the Cincinnati Reds won the NL West.

The Dodgers had a big year in 1977. They won the Western division easily.

Garvey only hit .297, an off year for him. But he hit 33 homers and 115 RBIs. Defensively he was as good as ever. He only had eight errors all season. The guy who couldn't make it at third base gained the NL record for fewest errors by a first baseman. He was awarded the Golden Glove award for the fourth straight season.

Los Angeles won the National League championship. They beat the Philadelphia Phillies three games to one. The Dodgers met the New York Yankees in the World Series. Steve Garvey batted .375 in the Series to lead his club. The Yankees won the Series in six games.

The Dodgers and Steve Garvey were back on top in 1978. In the All-Star game Steve had two RBIs in the third inning. He scored the winning run in the eighth after hitting a triple. For the second time, he was chosen the Most Valuable Player. Los Angeles won 22 of their last 37 games to clinch the Western Division title. Garvey hit .430 in September to help out. His average for the season was .316 with 21 homers and 113 RBIs. He had 202 hits, the highest in the National League.

Again the Dodgers faced the Philadelphia Phillies in the NL championship Series. In the first game of the Series, Garvey belted two home runs and drove in four runs. The Dodgers won it 9-5. The Phillies and the Dodgers split the next two games. In game number four Garvey slammed his fourth homer of the Series. It was Steve's 12th run scored in NL championship competition. That broke Pete Rose's mark of 11. The Dodgers won that game, 4-3, in the last half of the 10th inning. Los Angeles won the pennant three games to one. But L.A. couldn't handle the New York Yankees in the World Series. They lost in six games.

As for Steve Garvey, he'll be back. He loves the game. He loves the fans. He loves the team. Remember, he was born a Dodger!

Dave Parker

Baseball people used to say that Dave Parker would someday become the best big man in the game. Now they say that Parker will be the best player in baseball. That is, if he isn't there already.

"There's nothing Parker can't do on the field," his manager, Pittsburgh's Chuck Tanner, said recently. "There isn't a big man alive who can run with him, there are only a few who can field and throw with him, and for sheer consistency at bat, he does it all."

The talented Parker has always been big. He weighed 11 pounds, 14 ounces when he was born. (Most babies weigh about seven pounds.) Once a Cincinnati truant officer saw Dave playing outside. He thought the boy should be in school. The officer marched to the Parker's door and asked his mother for Dave's excuse. "He's only four years old," Mrs. Parker told the officer.

Years later when Dave reported to the Pirates' spring camp in 1971, Pittsburgh slugger Willie Stargell couldn't believe his eyes. "I couldn't picture anybody that big being so young," said Stargell, of the 19-year old Parker. And Stargell, no small person himself, was not alone. It was Parker's large 6'5", 235-pound frame that attracted scouts to the Cincinnati athlete in the first place.

When Parker was a student at Heinold Junior High and Courter Tech High School, his favorite sport was football. "Football was my first love," he said later. "I loved it because it was a contact game. I was like a big brute in high school. I liked to run over people."

Because of his size, he didn't have much trouble. He developed into a fine high school running back. He also played catcher on the Courter Tech baseball team. Unfortunately, Parker injured his knee during his junior year. His football career ended. After struggling through a so-so senior baseball season, Parker was a question mark in the draft. The Pirates finally took him in the 14th round of the 1970 draft.

"I signed for $6,500," he recalled later. "But if it wasn't for my bad knee, I probably would have been picked in the first or second round. It cost me about $90,000 or $95,000."

The Pirate organization soon found out Parker's knee was okay. He reported to Bradenton, Florida, with the rest of the rookie signees. He promptly won the 60-yard dash from the others in a time of 6.8. He has since run the same distance as fast as 6.3. The Pittsburgh managers saw Parker's speed. They decided that Parker's future in the big leagues wasn't as a catcher. He was handed a fielder's glove and told to play the outfield.

"Some of those fly balls almost hit me

on the head," said Parker, talking about his early days in the outfield. But his hitting was good. The Pirates gave the young slugger time to learn to play outfield.

Unlike many beginners, Parker started strong for the Pirates' rookie league farm club. He had a .314 average with four home runs. Pittsburgh next jumped him two notches to its Class AA team in Waterbury for the 1971 season. The jump proved to be a mistake for the Pirates, but in the end it helped Parker's career.

He hit only .228 in 30 games with the Eastern League club. Parker was sent down to Monroe in the Western Carolina League. There he got back on track. He hit .358 with 11 homers in 71 games. The Pittsburgh management decided that he had a great future ahead.

"I think the time in Waterbury helped me," he said, looking back on those days, "Because I knew I had a lot of work in front of me. I knew I had a lot of work left."

He was back on the Class A level in

1972. This time he won player of the year honors in the Carolina League. He led the league in hitting (.310) and runs batted in (101). He belted 22 home runs.

Chuck Tanner got his first glimpse of the huge outfielder in spring training in 1972. Tanner was managing the Chicago White Sox at that time. Tanner saw Parker in an exhibition game. Tanner went straight to Pittsburgh General Manager Joe Brown. "I told him he could have any player on the White Sox major league roster for Parker," Tanner recalled. "But Joe wouldn't think about it."

Parker belted Class AAA pitching at Charleston in 1973. His .317 batting mark was good enough to give him a shot with the big club later in the season. He hit .288 with the Pirates in his first 54 games. He had arrived in the majors.

The only question that remained was where Parker would play. The Pirates club still wasn't sure he should play outfield. The club had an opening at first base in 1974. The Pirates put Parker there. The experiment ended when management decided he was better in the outfield. Unfortunately, he didn't play much in the outfield that season. A series of pulled hamstring muscles kept him out of the lineup. In his first full season in the majors Parker played in only 73 games. His .282 batting mark wasn't bad. But Parker thought he could do much better.

"My main aim is to maintain a .300 average," Parker would repeat, every time reporters asked him why a man of his size didn't hit more homers. Although the huge left-hander had some difficulty with southpaw pitchers early in 1975, he quickly overcame that problem. He went on a hitting streak that put him in a class with the best young batters in the game.

The fans were delighted. Parker was enjoying it just as much as they were. He returned in mid-season to his hometown for a game with the Reds. His family and friends showed up to see him play. He responded with a three-run homer, a double and single.

"I've never lacked confidence," he said. "But this year is wiping out any

doubts."

There really was no reason for him to have any doubts. He completed the season with a .308 batting mark. He had 25 home runs and 101 runs batted in. He hit all of those homers without swinging for home runs at all. It was a true show of strength.

"There is no telling how many home runs Parker will hit when he reaches his peak," said then Pittsburgh Pirates' Manager Danny Murtaugh. But Parker continued to insist that he was swinging for nothing but hits.

"I aim to hit the ball hard," said Parker. "I'm not looking for the seats when I swing."

He played all of the 1976 season. But he played with a knee injury he received in mid-May. The Pirates couldn't afford to be without him. The injury kept him from performing at his best form.

His home run and RBI production suffered. He still managed to up his batting average for the season to .313. And his 13 home runs and 90 RBIs weren't too bad.

Scouts predicted that Dave would end up being an all-around superstar winning batting titles and having a high home run output at the same time. He finally proved that in 1977. That was to be the season that Parker finally reached stardom in all phases of the game.

First, there was tremendous improvement of his outfield skills. Parker worked hard to improve in that area. The results were astounding. He learned to use his shotgun arm and lightning speed. Parker polished his fielding skills enough to lead the league in assists with 26. He was even honored with the Gold Glove Award. This award is given annually to the best fielding player at each position in each league.

His hitting was even more important than his fielding. Parker put together two separate batting streaks of 22 games each. He won a starting position on the National League All-Star team. He maintained a .338 average. And he won the National League hitting title that he so wanted. He led the league in hits (215) and doubles (44). He smashed 21 home runs.

"Parker could be the best big man who ever played the game," said Chuck Tanner. "I haven't seen them all, but in my 30 years in baseball, I've never run across anyone who is as good as he is."

In 1978 the Pirates began poorly. Not Parker. He hit .334 to win the hitting title for the second year in a row. He led the Pirates in a late season comeback effort. During September Parker hit .419. The Pirates won 41 out of their last 54 games, but they ended up second to the Phillies.

"You knew he was something special," the late Danny Murtaugh once said, "He reminded me of (Roberto) Clemente, (Willie) Stargell...I can't think of too many others."

That's because there aren't too many others in Dave Parker's class. And he still has years to play.

Lou Brock

Lou Brock, the St. Louis Cardinals' 39-year old outfielder, inched his usual three and one-half steps off first base. His eyes were glued on San Diego pitcher Dave Freisleben. Freisleben threw to first. Brock got back easily. The 19,656 Padres' fans booed. They weren't booing Brock. They were booing their own pitcher. They were afraid Freisleben would keep them from seeing an important baseball event. Brock again moved off the base. His eyes followed Freisleben. Everyone knew what would follow. No one wanted to miss it. Freisleben threw the ball toward the plate. Brock made a mad dash to second. Catcher Dave Roberts threw to the right of the base. Shortstop Bill Almon grabbed the ball. It wasn't in time to nip the sliding Brock.

On August 29, 1977 Lou Brock had finally stolen his 893rd base. He was the number one base stealer in the history of the sport. "I knew it was going to happen," said Brock later. "I got the feeling that it didn't matter when it happened."

The fans who turned up that night had come with the hope of seeing Brock beat Ty Cobb's career mark of 892 steals. They knew he needed two steals to set a new mark. Brock led off the game with a walk and then stole his 892nd base. The fans knew they had a chance to see a historic moment. Even Freisleben was touched by the event. "I kind of got goose bumps," Freisleben said later.

After he broke the record, the crowd cheered. His St. Louis teammates mobbed him. But Brock was concerned with something else. He had crashed into

short stop Almon. He wanted to make sure the Padre infielder was O.K. "He took me out like on a double play," said Almon after the game. "He hit me pretty hard, he was afraid he'd spiked me. He asked me if I was O.K. Here he is, he's just set the record and is turning around showing concern. That's just the type of person he is."

When Brock broke Ty Cobb's record, he became the holder of almost every base stealing record that exists in major league baseball. He had come a long way since he began stealing bases with the St. Cloud, Minnesota team of the Class A Northern League.

Brock was born in Eldorado, Arkansas. He was raised in Collinston, Louisana. One of nine children, he was an outstanding all-around athlete at Merl Rouge's Union High School in Louisiana. He played three years of high school basketball. He pitched and played outfield on the baseball team. He hit .536 as a switch-hitting senior for Union. He then went on to attend Southern University in Baton Rouge. At Southern Brock studied mathematics and played baseball. He was named to the All-Southwestern Athletic Conference Team in

1959 and 1960. He also played on the Pan American Baseball Team in 1959. In 1961, he batted .352 for his college team and earned a bonus offer from the Chicago Cubs.

His minor league career was brief. After signing with the Cubs, Brock went first to St. Cloud. He began his professional baseball career by slugging the first pitch thrown at him for a home run. He still thinks of that as his greatest baseball thrill.

That was only the beginning of his hitting power. In that first season he hit .361 in 128 games. He won the Northern League batting championship. He also hit 14 home runs. He had 82 RBIs and stole 38 bases. He proved right away that he was worth every penny of the $30,000 bonus that he received.

He was so good that the Cubs brought him up to the major league team at the end of his first season of professional ball. He played in only four games and collected one hit in 11 at bat. In 1962, the 22-year old Brock became a starting outfielder for the Cubs. He hit only .263 in 1962 and .258 in 1963. In 1964 the Cubs traded Brock for pitcher Ernie Broglio. It was one of the worst deals in baseball history. Broglio, once a fine pitcher, had a sore arm. He won only four against seven losses for the Cubs. Brock became the key to a St. Louis pennant drive. In 103 games Brock hit an amazing .348. He had 12 home runs, 44 RBIs and 33 stolen bases. He has been a Cardinal star ever since.

Stan Musial, the retired St. Louis Cardinal star, knew the trade would work. "The Cardinals couldn't have won it with me in left field," said Musial. "And with this kid Brock we are going to win." Musial was right. The Cardinals nosed out Philadelphia and Cincinnati. They won the 1964 National League Pennant on the last day of the season. They also won pennants in 1967 and 1968. Brock led the way. He was a solid .290 hitter throughout these years. He finished second to Maury Wills in 1965 with 63 steals. Brock won the National

League stolen base crown the next four years.

"The most important thing about base stealing is not stealing the base," Brock said, "But disturbing the pitcher's concentration. If I can do that, then the hitter can get a better pitch to swing at and I will get a better chance to steal."

"I have a slight advantage over the pitcher because I can change my stealing technique while the pitcher's motion is mechanical. He can't alter it without risking injury to his arm." Brock takes advantage of that edge time and time again.

In important situations, Brock is at his best. In the 1967 World Series he stole seven bases and hit .414. In the 1968 World Series he again stole seven bases and hit .464. That tied the World Series base stealing mark of 14. No one has broken it yet. "He is a one-man offense," said first baseman Joe Torre during the World Series of 1968.

Brock stole more bases than any other major league player each year from 1966

to 1969. In 1970 Cincinnati's Bobby Tolan grabbed the stolen base title. But Brock regained his position. He was the leading base stealer again from 1971 through 1974.

1974 was his greatest base stealing season. The 35-year old Brock set out to beat Maury Wills' mark of 104 stolen bases in a single year. Lou began the 1974 season badly. On opening night he was thrown out in his first steal attempt of the season. But then he was off and running. He stole 28 straight bases before being cut down again. All season long he continued to steal.

Finally, on September 10, 1974, Brock was just one steal short of Wills' record. That night Brock stood ready on first base. The fans sensed what they were about to see. "Go, go go! " they chanted. Brock went on the second pitch. He stole second cleanly to tie Wills' record at 104. Now the Cardinal fans wanted to see the record broken. In the seventh inning, the 35-year old thief gave them their wish. He singled. He again waited only one pitch before making his run. The pitcher could have nailed him with a good throw. But he was confused by Brock's daring. The throw was wide. Brock had the record.

Brock was modest and relieved after he

broke the record. "I never thought it could happen," said Lou, after the game. "Now I'm glad it's over." Actually it wasn't over. Brock went on to steal 13 more bases in the final months of the 1974 season. He finished with 118 steals. His record seems even more unbreakable than Wills' "unbreakable" mark set in 1962. Brock doesn't believe in unbreakable records. "I look for someone to steal 150 bases before too long," he has said.

In 1976 the left-handed Brock again hit over .300. He also stole 56 bases that year.

Brock is now approaching retirement. His batting average for 1978 slumped below the .200 mark. But he still leads the all-time World Series left handed batters with .391 batting average. When he retires, he will almost certainly be elected to the Baseball Hall of Fame as soon as he is eligible. He is, after all, the greatest base stealer to come along so far.

Johnny Bench

Johnny Lee Bench is the best defensive catcher the sport has ever produced. He combines his catching with a powerful home run hitting strength. When he ends his career, he will likely have hit more home runs than any other catcher in the game's history. That includes the great Yogi Berra of the magnificent New York Yankee teams of the 50's and 60's. Bench is so good he is a sure bet to be elected to the Baseball Hall of Fame in the first year that he is eligible.

Johnny Bench was born in Oklahoma City, Oklahoma on December 7, 1947. He was raised in Binger, a small Oklahoma town with only 600 residents. His father, Ted Bench, had been an outstanding athlete himself. But when Ted Bench returned from World War II, he was too old to begin playing professional baseball. He had played catcher. Johnny could play all positions well, but his father constantly encouraged him to become a catcher.

"He kept telling me that catching was the quickest way to the majors because that's what they needed," Bench would recall again and again. "And I've been planning on being in the majors since I was in first grade."

The town of Binger had no little league teams. When Johnny was old enough to begin playing, his father organized a team of his own. He couldn't get enough people for a league. So Ted Bench drove the team 18 miles to Fort Cobb to play in the league there. Johnny quickly established himself as the team star. He played pitcher and catcher. He batted in the clean-up position (4th in the lineup).

In high school, Johnny starred in two

sports. He earned honorable mention All-American honors as a basketball guard. He pitched his baseball team to the Oklahoma championship. Major league scouts were impressed with Bench's ability. The Cincinnati Reds made the 6', 200-pound Bench their number two choice in the June 1965 draft.

Bench was assigned to Cincinnati's rookie league club in Tampa, Florida. The day after Johnny signed, he boarded a plane for Tampa. From the airport he went straight to the ball park. He arrived at the beginning of the ninth inning. The manager didn't hesitate to put him in. He explained, "You're the regular catcher from now on — in fact, you're the only catcher we have."

Johnny was a 17-year old country boy. He had some trouble adjusting to baseball life that first summer. He hit only two home runs in 68 games. He had a batting average of .248. The next year he was assigned to the Reds Class A club at Peninsula (New Port News) in the Carolina League. He began to show signs in, and a .275 average. He began the season in the seventh spot in the Cincinnati batting order. As the season progressed, he moved toward the top of the batting order. Finally he was hitting in the clean-up spot on one of the best hitting teams in the majors.

By the end of the 1968 season, he had also convinced most runners not to try to steal against him. Many tried to steal on the rookie and failed. With his shotgun arm, he led the league in catcher assists.

When the post season awards were handed out, he was the clear choice as National League Rookie of the Year—the first catcher ever to win it. He became the first rookie catcher to win the Gold Glove Award. This award goes to the best defensive player for each position. He was also chosen as a National League All-Star.

During spring training before his rookie season, Bench had met baseball's slugging great Ted Williams, at Pompano Beach, Florida. Williams, then manager of the Washington Senators, autographed a ball for Johnny. 'To Johnny Bench, a Hall of Famer for sure', wrote Williams. Bench cherishes that ball to this day.

Williams saw Bench during the 1969 season. He probably knew then that his prediction would come true. Johnny improved in almost all of his batting statistics. He knocked in 26 home runs. He drove in 90 runs and hit .293. He also continued his outstanding defensive play. Even his teammates were amazed by his throwing abilities. Teammate Woodie Woodward described the flight of a ball when Bench threw to second base. "You see the ball coming in low, and you are sure you are going to have to one-hop it. But it keeps right on coming. It explodes on you." Bench was chosen for the All-Star team. The first time he came to bat in the All-Star game he hit a homer.

1970 was a great season for Johnny Bench. With Sparky Anderson as their new manager, the 1970 Reds started the season by winning 70 out of their first 100 games. Bench was the main reason. He

tied a National League record for most home runs up through July 31 by hitting 36 homers. He went on to lead the League in homers (45) and runs batted in (148). And again he batted .293.

With Bench hitting, the Reds easily won the National League West title. Bench then hit another homer to help Cincinnati defeat Pittsburgh for the National League pennant. The Reds lost the World Series to Baltimore in five games. But Bench won the National League's Most Valuable Player honors. Sparky Anderson spoke of Bench in glowing terms. "They talk about the Messiah coming back," Sparky once told a group of reporters. "I'm not sure he hasn't already returned. I mean Johnny Bench."

But 1971 was an off year for Johnny. His home run total dropped to 27 and his RBIs to 61. He hit .238. It was a poor season for Bench and for the Reds. Critics and sports writers began to ask, what happened? Had Bench lost his power? Had he lost enthusiasm for the game?

Bench was sure he hadn't. He proved it the following season.

The 1972 Reds were a different club. Three new players—Joe Morgan, Jack Billingham, and Cesar Geronimo—had been acquired from Houston. Bench was a different man at the plate too. The 24-year old veteran regained his home run power. He again hit more home runs (40) and had more RBIs (125) than any other player in the National League. Cincinnati again took the National League West Crown in 1972. The Reds met the World Champion Pittsburgh Pirates in the National League playoffs.

After the first four games each club had won two. In the ninth inning of the fifth and final game, the Pirates were leading 3-2. Pirate Manager Bill Virdon sent in his best relief pitcher, Dave Guisti, to finish the game. The first hitter to face Guisti was Bench. He stepped up to the plate. He hit a long homer that tied the game. Cincinnati then went on to score another run to win the game. "This has to be the thrill of my baseball life," said a happy Bench after the game. Although the Reds lost the World Series to Oakland that year, Bench was again named the National League's Most Valuable Player.

Bench was on top again. At least, that is what the public thought. But during the 1972 season, doctors had discovered a spot on Johnny's right lung. After post-season play was over, the doctors decided surgery was necessary. Bench was operated on in December. The growth was non-cancerous. Johnny Bench was told he could continue his baseball career. In fact, he would be ready to play when the 1973 season started.

And play he did in 1973. It was not a spectacular season for Johnny. He hit 25 homers and 104 RBIs. His batting average was .253. But as one writer said, "He had an amazing year when you consider the surgery he underwent last December."

In 1974 Johnny Bench showed everyone he was 100 percent once again. He led the National League in runs batted in with 129. He hit 33 home runs and batted .280. Bench had a good year. But the Reds weren't good enough to beat the Dodgers for the Western Division crown.

Then came the 1975 season. The Reds could not be stopped. Cincinnati clinched the Western Division title on September 7th. No team had ever won a title that early. Johnny's batting average was .283.

The Reds, known as "The Big Red Machine", met the Boston Red Sox in the World Series. Everyone agreed that the two teams were the best in baseball. Game one belonged to the Red Sox. In game two the Reds were down 2-1. In the top of the ninth, Bench hit a double. That started a rally. Johnny scored and tied the game. Then Ken Griffey's double gave the Reds the go ahead run. After four games, the teams had won two games each. The Big Red Machine went on to win the Series in seven games. Johnny Bench's work in the field was one of the reasons. He not only helped call the pitches, but also made several outstanding throws to second base.

Bench had hit 25 or more homers every season until 1976. That year he had personal and physical problems. Even that year his defensive play was excellent. And in the World Series, he proved he hadn't lost his hitting ability. He almost single-handedly beat the New York Yankees. He hit two homers, drove in six runs and collected eight hits for a .533 average in the four-game sweep of the Yankees. He earned the Series Most Valuable Player award. Cincinnati won a second consecutive World Championship.

Bench continued his hard hitting in the 1977 season. He belted 31 homers and drove in 109 runs. Shoulder problems and a back injury bothered him. Bench continued to dig bad pitches out of the dirt, down runners at second and knock in home runs.

In 1978 Johnny Bench again was selected for the All-Star game. But he couldn't play due to a bad back. His back bothered him all season. He only batted .260.

He remains today one of the game's great power hitters and defensive players. He is clearly the "Best Catcher in the Game". Sparky Anderson, the former Manager of the Reds, explains over and over, "There is Bench and then there is everyone else." But it was Cincinnati outfielder Alex Johnson who best described Johnny's ability. Alex was sitting next to Bench's locker when a group of writers came into the clubhouse looking for the Reds' catcher. "Where did Bench go?", one of the writers asked Johnson politely. Alex didn't bat an eye.

"Probably to a higher league!," said Johnson. There may not be a league high enough for Johnny Bench.

Mike Schmidt

Mike Schmidt's life has been marked by a series of miracles and comebacks.

When he was only seven years old, he was climbing a tree in the backyard of his Dayton, Ohio home. He had climbed 30 feet in the air when the branch broke. He reached out and grabbed a power wire to keep from falling to the ground. The wire carried 4,000 volts of electricity. Mike managed to let go of the wire and dropped to the ground. He could have been killed, or at least seriously injured. But the charge went through his body and came out his shins. "I was down for about five months and the doctors said that I was double lucky that I didn't break my neck or anything else in the fall," recalls Schmidt. He still has two scars on his shins, but they have never hurt his athletic ability.

Mike was a three-sport star at Fairview High School in Dayton, Ohio. He played baseball, football, and basketball. He played shortstop on the baseball team. He was the football team's quarterback, linebacker and punt returner as a sophomore. In his first game that year, he was hit on the knee while returning a punt. Knee troubles began then. He still managed to play basketball. He also continued as shortstop on the baseball team. The following fall, he could play in only three football games. As promising as Mike was as an athlete, the knee problems were ruining his chances for a pro sports career.

"The doctors think there could have been a weakness in my knee from the high wire accident," Mike explained later. Most pro scouts and college scouts shy away from athletes with weak knees.

Schmidt enrolled at Ohio University to study architecture. But athletic ambitions aren't easily forgotten. Mike soon tried out for, and made, the freshman basketball team. Unfortunately, Schmidt again had knee problems. This time university officials, not a doctor, gave Mike the bad news. The university could not cover his shaky knees in their insurance plan. The risk was too high.

But Mike refused to give up. He started lifting weights to strengthen his knees. He began at five pounds. He worked his way to 90-pound weights. His knees were again strong enough to participate in sports.

Baseball wasn't as hard on the knees as basketball. University officials reluctantly allowed him to try out for baseball. He became the star of Coach Bob Wren's Bobcat Club. He was the slugging shortstop on an Ohio University club that advanced to the College World Series in Omaha, Nebraska. As a junior, he was already an All-American. "I could have signed for a bundle then," said

Schmidt, later. "But I wasn't old enough."

Although his senior year wasn't quite as good as the previous season, Schmidt was chosen by the Philadelphia Phillies, No. 2 in the 1971 free agent draft.

He began his pro career at Reading, Pennsylvania, hitting only eight home runs and having only a .211 average. However, the Phillies thought enough of him to promote him to the Eugene, Oregon Class AAA Pacific Coast League in 1972. He struck out 145 times that season. But he also gave the Phillies the first real look at his power. He slammed 26 home runs. He drove in 91 runs and hit for a .291 average.

At the end of the season, the management brought Schmidt up from the minor leagues. He was given a chance to try out for the parent team. Before the 1973 season started, Don Money was traded to Milwaukee. Twenty-three-year old Schmidt became the regular third baseman.

If that sounds like the happy ending to

a long, frustrating story, it wasn't. In some ways, Schmidt's troubles had just begun. After a fine spring training, the new Philadelphia third baseman threw his shoulder out. He missed the entire first month of the season.

He finally returned to the lineup. But his batting average suffered. He did hit 18 home runs. But he struck out 136 times. His average slumped to .196. Everybody in the Phillies' organization tried to tell him how to hit. Why couldn't everyone just leave hime alone?

Schmidt went to Puerto Rico that winter. There, he learned to hit the ball out of the park without swinging from the heels. The lesson straightened Mike out mentally. But he still had one difficulty yet to face.

At spring training in 1974 everyone began to give him advice all over again. This time Schmidt answered his helpers with his bat. "I stopped acting as though every trip to the plate was a life-or-death proposition," Mike said. "Instead of trying to hit every pitch with every ounce of strength, I tried to pick out a good pitch and swing naturally letting the home runs take care of themselves." Six

months later Mike was the National League home run champion with 36 homers. He had a .282 average and 116 runs batted in. In his second year of major league play, Schmidt had become one of baseball's brightest slugging stars. And he had done it on his own.

His success didn't stop there either. 1975 was another good year for Mike. He did have a problem with strikeouts that year, 180. But for the second year in a row, he proved himself to be a great home run hitter. He led the National League with 58 home runs. "When I was a kid, I always wanted to crush the ball," Mike recalls. "I know that I shouldn't take the long strike and the big swing," he says. "I **know** that I should just try to meet the ball. But knowing these things isn't enough. It's a matter of learning mentally to discipline yourself."

Schmidt's power as a home run hitter was not his only talent. He finished second in the Gold Glove voting for third basemen. Mike also stole 29 bases.

At the start of 1976, the Phillies' third

baseman was third in the batting order. But, early in the year his batting average dropped below the .200 mark. Manager Danny Ozark dropped Mike from his No. 3 spot to No. 6. Schmidt was not happy.

In the first game after the switch, the Phillies played the Chicago Cubs. The Cubs took an early 13-2 lead. Schmidt singled in the fourth. Then he cleared Wrigley Field's leftfield wall with a two-run homer in the fifth. The game was still apparently out of reach. Then Mike slammed another ball over the leftfield wall in the seventh. He hit a two-run homer over the centerfield wall in the eighth. Finally, in the tenth, with the game now tied, Schmidt struck again. He lined a fast ball into the left centerfield seats with a man on base. Philadelphia won the game 18-16. Schmidt had slammed four home runs in a row.

"I don't think it would have made any difference where I batted," said Schmidt, after the game. "When the Cubs got so far ahead, I think I just relaxed and started swinging the bat."

He kept right on swinging too. He clobbered home runs in each of the Phillies' next three games. In all he hit seven homers in four games. That was only one short of Ralph Kiner's incredible eight homers in four games in 1947.

Unlike many big leaguers, the modest Schmidt didn't let the four-homer day go to his head. In fact, it was just the opposite. "When a batter strikes out four times in a game," said Schmidt, "they tell him to forget it. Well, I'd like to forget about the homers and concentrate on the games ahead. Maybe after the season, I'll look back and think about it."

Schmidt and the rest of the Phillies concentrated on the games ahead. That year, 1976, they gave Philadelphia its first baseball title since 1950. Unfortunately, the Cincinnati Reds swept the Phillies three straight in the National League playoffs. But Schmidt had won the batting title for the third year in a row with 38 home runs.

1977 was a frustrating season for Mike Schmidt. He started the season with a leg injury. Still, he slugged 14 home runs in June. And by the end of July, he had hit 25 homers to take over the major league lead. But then he fractured his finger. He ended the season with 38 homers. But Mike didn't even come close to winning his fourth straight National League home run crown. Cincinnati outfielder George Foster belted 52 homers. At third base that season Schmidt was outstanding. He received the Gold Glove award.

Mike's batting average stuck around the .250 mark throughout the early part of the 1978 season. His home run totals also dropped. Again he was injured. He strained a hamstring muscle in his right leg. Some critics even began to wonder if Mike Schmidt's days were over—even before he was 30. Schmidt didn't think so.

Schmidt said, "I'm not worried as long as I'm swinging the bat good. Individual statistics aren't that important. We're all trying to get into the World Series and everything else is incidental."

Schmidt even went to the Phillies'

leadoff spot late in the 1978 season. Manager Danny Ozark wanted to help the club and to help pull Schmidt out of his slump at the same time. "It's different," said Schmidt. "I'm just trying to make contact and get on base, get some walks and hits and score some runs. I think in the long run the home runs will come." The Phillies won the National League East. But lost for the second year in a row in the playoffs to the Dodgers.

Schmidt is looking forward to 1979. With the addition of Pete Rose, the Phillies hope to finally get into the World Series. A healthy Mike Schmidt will certainly make a difference to the club. And as often as Mike has come back, he'll probably do it again.

Jim Rice

Jim Rice had been in the major leagues only a year and a half when baseball's all-time home run king paid him his highest compliment. Hank Aaron said that if anyone broke his all-time career home run mark of 755, it would probably be young Jim Rice.

"He is a lot stronger than I was at 21," said Aaron. "He is built like a bull. He has the natural ability and he has Fenway Park with its short leftfield wall. Once he learns to hit, he is going to hit a lot of home runs. He'll be hitting 40 a year."

Now Aaron's prediction doesn't seem

far off base. Rice hit 39 homers in 1977 to win his first home run crown. In 1978 he hit 46 homers. Boston baseball buffs are convinced that he has many more slugging records ahead. "I don't think there's a limit as to how good he can be," said his Boston Manager Don Zimmer. "With his 6'2", 200-pound build and his powerful bat, Rice looks forward to a bright future.

Jim Rice was born in Anderson, South Carolina. Growing up he starred in football, basketball, baseball and track. He could have earned a college scholarship in any one of the four sports. For a long time he didn't really think baseball was any more important than the others. Even today Rice enjoys other sports. When he is not playing baseball, he is often playing par golf.

Jim Rice chose baseball over other sports partly because of a man named John Moore. When Jim was an eighth grader playing on the school baseball team, he got sick and missed a week of classes. Jim returned to the team and gave no explanation for his absence. Moore said "no" to his return.

"When I came back, he wouldn't let me play," Rice explained later. "Now I really wanted to play and I kept coming around, begging to play. I've been playing ever since." That was when Rice became determined to become a major league baseball player.

He shows his determination now by spending more time in the batting cage than any other player on his squad. He always hits the ball with the greatest bat speed possible. If he hits with good bat speed, he knows the ball will travel great distances. Rice has incredible strength that is rare even among the most powerful hitters.

Jim Rice has been hitting home runs almost since the day he was chosen as the number one draft by the Boston Red Sox. When he graduated from high school, he went to Williamsport. He began playing Class A ball in the New York/Pennsylvania league. During his first season he hit only .256 with five home runs and 27 runs batted in. He has done better than that every season since.

In 1972, Rice blasted 17 homers, drove in 87 runs, and batted .292 for the Red Sox Class A Winter Haven Farm Club. His performance earned him honors as a league all-star.

In 1973 Rice moved up to Bristol to the Class AA Eastern League. Here Rice showed that he was more than just a power hitter. He won the batting title with a .317 average. He also hit 27 home runs, had 93 RBIs, and earned a spot on the Class AA National All-Star team. At the end of the 1973 season, he moved to the Red Sox Class AAA farm club at Pawtucket. The Paw Sox were driving for a pennant when Rice joined the club. Jim hit four home runs, drove in 10 runs and batted .378 in the final ten games. Pawtucket grabbed the league title. His three-run homer then clinched the title in the Little World Series championship over Tulsa.

Rice stayed with Pawtucket in 1974. When the International League season

ended, he was the International League triple crown winner. He led the league in home runs (25), runs batted in (93), and batting average (.337). Then he joined the major league Red Sox team. Rice played in 24 major league games at the end of the 1974 season. He drove in 12 runs, hit one homer and hit .269.

In 1975 Boston had been picked to finish no higher than third in the

American League East. But Jim Rice and his former Pawtucket teammate, outfielder Fred Lynn, both joined the team that year. Rice became the designated hitter because Boston had three excellent outfielders already. Lynn and Rice were primarily responsible for the Red Sox' American League pennant. They both turned in great rookie performances.

Lynn attracted most of the attention. The 23-year old University of Southern California graduate had a remarkable season, batting .331, knocking 21 homers, and driving in 105 runs. He played brilliantly in the field as well. When the year was completed, Lynn had scored a first. He was voted the American League's most valuable player. He was also chosen as Rookie of the Year.

In spite of Lynn's performance, it was difficult, even impossible to ignore the powerful Rice. He belted 22 home runs, drove in 109 runs, and batted .309. His statistics would have earned him rookie of the year honors in many other years. Half way through the year, Rice became the starting leftfielder. He worked hard and improved his fielding skills. He went through the last half of the season without an error.

For both Rice and Lynn, it was a story book rookie season. There was one disappointment. By the time the Red Sox had clinched the eastern division flag, Rice was out of action. A pitched ball hit his arm and broke it. His broken arm caused him to miss the Red Sox' upset victory over Oakland in the play-offs. He also missed the 1975 World Series which Cincinnati won in seven games. But Rice wasn't bitter.

"I'd love to play in the Series," said Rice later, "But I couldn't be upset with missing the last one. I'm happy God gave me the ability to get as far as I did. The man wasn't throwing at me, the ball just ran in. It's part of the game."

In his second year, Jim Rice avoided the "sophomore jinx" that often bothers young players. He blasted 25 home runs, drove in 85 runs and hit .282. He played again as designated hitter. Jim was an above average fielder. But he still couldn't crack the Boston outfield of Carl Yastrzemski, Fred Lynn, and Dwight Evans. "We've got a lot of stars on this team," Rice repeated time after time. "My day will come."

In 1977 the Red Sox finished in a tie for second place. Rice became the strongest designated hitter the league has seen. He won the American League Home Run Crown with 39 homers. He drove in 114 runs. He hit .320.

At the close of the '77 season, Boston Manager Don Zimmer explained Rice's improvement. "In '75 and '76, Rice used to chase outside breaking balls and normally if the pitcher didn't make mistakes, he'd get him out. Now I wouldn't want to be pitching to him. He's hitting good pitches, bad pitches, just about everything."

In 1978 Rice improved even more. He again won the home run title with 46 homers. He also led the majors in runs batted in (139), hits (213), triples (15) and slugging percentage (.600). And he got his homers when his team needed them. Thirty of his homers either tied games or gave his team the lead. He also was the first American League player since Joe DiMaggio to account for over 400 bases

in one season.

With Rice leading the way, the Red Sox won the last eight games of the 1978 season. They tied the New York Yankees for the American League East title. Then they lost in the one game playoff to the powerful New York team.

Even though Boston has several outstanding players—Carl Yastrzemski, Carlton Fisk, Fred Lynn and George Scott, Rice has become the star of stars. Fans in Boston love him. He is, in fact, the first Black player to become a superstar in Boston.

Tales of Jim Rice's super human strength have helped create his superstar image. Zimmer tells an amazing Rice story. "I was the first base coach, we were in Detroit and Rice was up. He had a one and two count on him and the pitcher threw him a low outside slider which was outside the strike zone. Jim went for it and got the bat as far as home plate, when he saw it was a bad pitch and held up. The bat snapped off about three inches above the hands. He had the handle left in his hands and the barrel of the bat flew over in front of the Detroit dug-out. I couldn't believe what had happened."

Because Rice is so strong, he can hit homers no matter where the ball is pitched. Unlike most home run hitters, Rice is not a pull-hitter. "I've never been a pull-hitter," said Rice. "A lot of people hit the ball hardest when you pull it; I hit the ball hardest when I go to the center or right center. Some of the hardest home runs I've ever hit have been to the opposite field." This explains why Rice has been able to have such a high batting average and so many homers at the same time.

When Rice was selected as the 1978 American League's Most Valuable Player, he was thrilled but humble. "Just because you win the MVP one year doesn't mean you have established yourself. I've got to do it every year."

That sounds like a tough order. But Jim Rice will probably do it!

Reggie Jackson

Storm clouds have surrounded Reggie Jackson throughout his major league baseball career, but the New York Yankee slugger has always managed to override them with his own brand of home run thunder.

Although he has played in the major leagues for 12 years, Jackson is still misunderstood by fans and players. Jackson speaks out on anything and everything. He always turns up in the limelight. From the day he first put on a baseball uniform he has been a headline-grabber.

Jackson was a high school All-American in both baseball and football. He continued to attract attention at Arizona State University. There he again played both sports. He was a college All-American in baseball with 15 runs batted in and a .327 average. He was the first college player to hit a ball out of Phoenix Municipal Stadium (he hit it an estimated 480 feet).

The Kansas City Athletics made him the first pick in the 1966 free agent draft. He signed for a $90,000 bonus — his first big money. He went to Lewiston of the Northwest League. He quickly moved to Modesto in the California circuit. There, he hit a remarkable 21 homers in 56 games. He also had one game where he hit three home runs.

In the Class AA league the following season, he slugged 17 homers and drove in 58 runs. He spent less than two seasons in the minor leagues. Even though he had been named Southern League Player of The Year, the minors really didn't suit his showy style.

The Kansas City Athletics moved to

Oakland in 1968. That year the 22-year old first-year slugger quickly became a star. While the A's dropped to sixth place in the American League, Jackson socked 29 home runs — fourth best in the league. He was becoming one of the best power hitters in the league. He also led the American League in strikeouts with 171, a problem that he still battles today.

Reggie started his second season hitting lots of home runs. He had 37 home runs at the mid-season All-Star break. The news media began following his attempt to top Roger Maris' record of 61 home runs in one season. Maris had broken Babe Ruth's long held record of 60 homers in 1961.

Reggie went into a slump after that. He hit only 10 homers the rest of the year and finished with 47. Oddly enough, he has never been close to that figure again.

"Even though I hit all of those home runs, I didn't feel like another Babe Ruth," said Jackson. "I was just hot and in the groove and the home runs were coming."

Harmon Killebrew hit 49 homers that year for Minnesota, so Reggie didn't even lead the American League in homers. But it was a pretty fair season for a man who was only in his second full year in the majors. And he did accomplish several other things that season.

Jackson recalls a game in Boston that year as one of his all-time favorites. Oakland scored 21 runs that day on 25 hits. Jackson's performance was one of the greatest individual feats ever. He had two homers, two doubles and a single — 5 for 6. He also drove in 10 runs, one short of the all-time record. The only time he didn't hit, he struck out — with the bases loaded, no less.

In 1970, Jackson slumped. His home run and RBI figures were cut nearly in half. He belted only 23 home runs and drove in only 66 runs. His average fell from .275 to .237. Many critics felt that Jackson had merely had a single surprising season. He improved in 1971 but did not have an outstanding year.

The fighting Oakland A's won the

pennant in 1972. But for Reggie, the season turned into the biggest disappointment of his career. In the final game of the AL play-offs against Detroit, Jackson came barreling toward the plate on the front-end of a double steal. It would have erased a 1-0 Tiger lead and put the A's in the game. Reggie picks up the story. "I was about 30 feet from the plate when I hurt myself," said Jackson. "I pulled a muscle. If I stopped, I would be out, but if I kept going it would tear up my leg. We needed the run to tie so I kept going."

He scored the run. The A's went on to win 2-1. But he had pulled a hamstring and stretched some ligaments in his knee. The A's won the 1972 World Series in seven games from the Cincinnati Reds. Jackson watched from the sidelines.

Jackson's best friend on the club, outfielder Joe Rudi, recalled how Reggie felt. "He was really down," said Rudi. "A guy plays a whole career waiting to play in a World Series and here was his chance and he was hurt."

The misfortune seemed to push Jackson to greater heights in 1973. The defending world champions charged toward their second AL West title in a row. Reggie had his best season at the plate since 1969. He smashed 32 homers, drove in 117 runs and hit .293.

There was a storybook ending to the season too. The A's made it to the World Series for the second season in succession. This time Jackson was healthy and ready to play. He was also pressing. Through his first 12 at-bats against the New York Mets, Reggie had only one hit. He seemed headed toward a terrible series until game number six. "I was thinking about last year," said Jackson, "I was thinking about being hurt, thinking about my legs, and I didn't produce."

In the sixth game Oakland was desperate. They were trailing the Mets three games to two. Tom Seaver was pitching for New York. Jackson ripped a pair of two-out RBI doubles. Oakland scored its first two runs. Then he singled and scored for a 3-1 win.

The A's went on to win the series. Jackson was named the series Most Valuable Player. Later he received an even greater honor. The American

League named him its Most Valuable Player for 1973. It had been a dream year. But like most great stars, Jackson still wasn't satisfied.

"I have not hit .300 yet," said Jackson. "I have not hit more than 50 home runs in a season, and I have not stolen more than 40 bases. There are lots of things that I can do in this game that I still haven't done. Until I do all of them, I will be shortchanging myself, the fans, the owners, the team and everybody else. I would like to be the best."

Since then Jackson has made a lot of money. He has also made a lot of enemies. And he hasn't accomplished his goals. But Reggie has managed to become one of the best drawing cards in the American League. The fans pack the stadiums to see him. They either love him or they hate him.

In 1974, Jackson got into a clubhouse fight with teammate Bill North. Catcher Ray Fosse tried to break it up. Fosse ended up on the disabled list. The fight wasn't good for Reggie's image.

The A's won the pennant that year. But several Oakland players were not pleased that Jackson was hogging most of the headlines. Reggie followed with a good season in 1975. He crashed 36 homers and drove in 104 runs. But he criticized A's owner Charlie Finley and some of the Oakland players. He kept things hopping all year.

He also refused to sign his contract. He went the free agent route, hoping for a big money contract. The A's knew they were going to lose him at the end of the 1976 season. They traded him to Baltimore before the season began. Reggie refused to report because he didn't want to play anywhere but on the West coast. His national fan club stopped growing. He was beginning to be known as a loudmouth troublemaker. Many fans thought he cared only for large sums of money and lots of press clippings. He finally reported to the Orioles early in the 1976 season. Many of the Baltimore players publicly criticized his behavior.

Oriole pitching ace Jim Palmer said,

"Reggie's not being here is psychologically destructive to the club. We gave up three quality players to get him. If we have to start the season without him, the first inclination is to ask, why did we make the trade?"

When Jackson finally reported he played well. He missed the first month of the season, but Reggie still ended the year with 27 home runs, 91 RBIs and a .277 average. He was a free agent at the season's conclusion. He signed a multi-year contract with the New York Yankees for a big salary. Reggie was back in the spotlight.

But Reggie became involved in more disagreements in New York than he ever had in Oakland. The Yankee club was called "the best team money can buy". Jackson was singled out by the fans and some of the players as the greedy villain. He couldn't get along with Yankee Manager Billy Martin. Jackson also criticized his teammates. His criticism created hard feelings among Yankee players. He always said what he thought.

The press printed it. Some of his teammates began to believe that Jackson was interested only in his press clippings.

Finally, Jackson gained the respect of some of his teammates. He helped the Yankees make it into the 1977 World Series. He turned in an incredible hitting performance in the Series. He had an even more amazing performance in one single World Series game.

Reggie slugged two homers in the first five games of the series with the Los Angeles Dodgers. He saved the best for last. After five games New York had won three. In the sixth game, Jackson slammed three straight home runs. He drove in five runs for the Yankees' 8-4 title-clinching victory. The only other three homer games in World Series competition belonged to none other than Babe Ruth. Ruth did it in 1926 and 1928. Jackson topped all marks with five homers in a single series.

"I have to admit that when Reggie hit his third home run and I was sure no one was watching, I applauded into my

glove," Los Angeles first baseman Ste Garvey said.

Similar praise poured in from both sides of the diamond. Even Yankee catcher Thurman Munson, who had been unable to get along with Jackson all year, praised Reggie. "Without him, we wouldn't have won the pennant," said Munson. "Without him we wouldn't have won the World Series." In a way, all was forgiven.

But in 1978 Reggie was back to his old tricks. He got into a fight with Yankee Manager Billy Martin. Worst of all, he did it in the dugout in front of national television cameras. Finally, Martin suspended Jackson for refusing to obey orders. Soon after, Martin was fired as Manager of the Yankees. Many fans felt that Jackson was responsible.

The 1978 season ended with the Yankees tied with the Boston Red Sox. In their one game tie-breaker, Jackson came to bat in the eighth inning and hit a home run which turned out to be the winning run.

He starred in the American League Championship Series against the Kansas City Royals. DH (designated hitter) Reggie Jackson had three hits including a home run. He also hit a homer in the third game. This helped the Yankees win the pennant for the second straight year.

The World Series put Jackson in the spotlight again. In the first game of the series, Reggie hit a home run into the Yankee bullpen, approximately 430 feet from home plate. It was Reggie's sixth home run in his last four Series games. This broke Lou Gehrig's World Series record. The Dodgers won the game 11-5. However, Reggie, who was referred to as Mr. October (the month of the Series), had only begun.

Game two the Yankees lost. They won game three 5-1. Game four had one of the most talked about plays in Series history. Jackson was at stage center. With the Dodgers leading 3-0 in the sixth inning, Reggie hit a single to drive in the first Yankee run. Then the big play happened. A ball was hit to the Dodger shortstop who forced Jackson at second base. The shortstop then threw to first in an effort to complete a double play. But, the ball hit Jackson in the leg and bounced away. Did Reggie let the ball hit him on purpose? If so, the double play was complete. The Dodgers complained. But the umpire ruled that Jackson had not blocked the throw on purpose, so another Yankee runner scored. The Yankees finally won the game 4-3. As Yankee Manager Bob Lemon said later, "Something odd always happens around Reggie."

New York won the fifth and sixth games to clinch the Series. The Yankees were the first team to win four straight Series games after losing two. And, Reggie was one of the main reasons they won. He finished the Series with eight RBIs and a batting average of .391. Most remarkable was the fact that in the past seven years, Reggie had played on four championship teams.

Reggie Jackson's future with the Yankees is anyone's guess. He is not known for his winning personality, but he has proved himself a superstar. And, as everyone will admit, there is only one "Reggie".

Rod Carew

If Rod Carew quit playing baseball tomorrow, he would still be elected to the Hall of Fame as soon as he was eligible. And he's only 32. Few Hall of Famers could have made that boast at that age. Carew is apart from the crowd. In modern baseball circles, Rod Carew stands alone.

What makes Carew different from other modern players? His batting average. It looks like a set of figures misplaced in time. Carew hits 1920's averages in the 1970's.

For over 30 years, baseball people have spoken of the .400 batting mark with reverence. No one has reached that figure since 1941. The man who made it that year, Ted Williams, is known as one of the best hitters in the history of the sport.

Carew hasn't reached that figure yet. But he has changed baseball attitudes about it. Until Carew came along, no one thought there could be a .400 hitter in the 1970's. The incredible batting figures of Ty Cobb, Honus Wagner, Rogers Hornsby and George Sisler — all from a distant era — no longer seem impossible.

"If he (Carew) gets lucky and stays healthy, I think he can hit .400," said then Twins' Manager Frank Quilici way back in 1974. "He has so many offensive gifts. He has great speed so he beats out a lot of hits. And when he isn't hitting, he can always bunt for hits. Now, after seven years in the league, he's found himself."

Found himself, indeed. Since Quilici made that statement, Carew's season batting averages have been .364, .359, .331, .388, and .333. Four of these were good enough for American League batting titles. Once he was just another good singles hitter in a power-hitter's game. Today he is recognized as the best hitter in baseball.

The Carew story has been unusual from the beginning. On October 1, 1945, his mother knew that her baby was due. She caught the train from Gatun, Panama to the city of Gamboa. She wanted to go to a clinic to have her baby. But the baby was in a hurry. A physician named Dr. Rodney Cline happened to be riding the train. He made the surprise delivery. As a way of thanking the doctor, the Carews named their boy Rodney Cline Carew.

Rod played baseball as a boy. When he was 12 he came down with rheumatic fever. After his illness, Rod's father ignored his weak, sickly son. As a result, Rod spend more and more time with his uncle, Joseph French. French was a Little League coach. He encouraged Rod to work on his baseball skills. He took him to games. He helped make Carew the player he is today.

The Panamanian boy won a bat — a Ted Williams' model — for outstanding play in the local Little League circuit. His prized possession was finally stolen after a pickup game. The loss of his bat almost broke the little boy's heart.

He had two childhood dreams while he was growing up in Panama: 1) he wanted to go to the United States and 2) he wanted to become a major league baseball player. He was to achieve both.

When Rod was 15, his mother moved to New York City. She found a place to live and a job. Then she sent for Rod and his older brother Eric. Rod had to work to help support his family. He didn't have time to play high school sports. He did sometimes play ball in sandlot games in a park next to Yankee Stadium. During one of the games there, he caught the eye of an unpaid scout of the Twins. The "scout" was the father of one of his teammates. He helped Rod get a tryout in Yankee Stadium when the Twins came to town.

The skinny 18-year old didn't look like

much when he entered the batting cage. In minutes he changed that impression. The Panamanian sandlot player kept drilling balls into the Yankee Stadium bleachers. Minnesota Manager Sam Mele couldn't believe his eyes. "Get him out of here before somebody sees the kid," Mele is reported to have said. They did. Carew signed with the Twins for a $5,000 bonus about a month later.

He was sent to the Twins' minor league team in Cocoa, Florida. There, he hit .325 in 37 games. His average was the second best in the league.

He spent only two more years in the minor leagues. Both years were on the Class A level. In the Florida State League in 1965, the young second baseman hit .303. He moved to the Twins' Wilson Carolina League club in 1966. He didn't exactly set the league on fire. He hit .292 with one home run. But Minnesota needed help at second base. Young Carew was given a chance to make the big club in 1967.

In his first season, 1967, Carew hit

.292. He matched his average in the Carolina League only a year before. He blasted eight home runs. He was chosen as the American League Rookie of the Year. If he hadn't ended the season 0 for 12, he might have finished with a .300 mark.

1968 wasn't as successful a year for Carew. His average dipped to .273. But that year he met his future wife, Marilynn Levy.

Until that time, Rod seemed to be a loner. He had been that way ever since he left Panama. He was rather moody. He couldn't handle criticism. Marilynn helped him feel better about himself.

He also worked hard to improve his hitting. In 1969 Rod Carew won his first American League batting title with a .332 average. One reason he won the title was his bunting.

Bunting has become something of a lost art among modern players. But Carew bunts and runs with lightening speed. During spring training Rod spends 45 minutes each day practicing his bunting. During the season he practices for 15 minutes before games. When he faces a pitcher who usually gives him trouble, Rod turns to his bunting ability. During 1972 he actually bunted safely 25 times in 36 attempts.

"Even when they know I'm going to bunt, they can't throw me out," said Carew. "I can drop the ball to a spot where they will have to make an awkward throw. They have to come up clean with the ball and throw on the run, and not too many third basemen can do that consistently."

His bunting goes with his peculiar hitting habits. He uses four different batting stances. He has two for right-handed pitchers and two for southpaws. He chooses his stance according to the pitcher's tactics. Most hitters never change their stance. They fear that changing will ruin their swing. Carew's stance-changing is most unusual, and it works.

After winning that first AL batting title in 1969, he has been as consistent as any hitter in baseball history. He has collected batting titles the way many batters collect strike-outs.

In 1970 he was hitting .376 until he suffered a knee injury. He returned to the lineup in September. He wound up hitting a league-leading .366. But he didn't have enough at bats to qualify for the league title. Since then, he has missed leading the American League in batting only once. That was in 1971 when he was out because of his knee injury.

Carew has come close to the .400 figure several times in his career. In 1974 he hit .400 midway through July only to finish at .364. But none of the years were comparable to his 1977 effort.

Carew attracted nation-wide attention by hanging close to the .400 mark throughout the season. He was hitting .401 as late as July 10. Between July 11 and August 25, his mark fell all the way to .374. Most baseball fans gave up on him during that stretch. Then during the month of September, he hit .436. That was good enough to raise his average to

.388, the highest batting mark since Ted Williams hit .388 in 1957. "Another week and I might have hit .400," he said when the season ended. And indeed he might have.

His 239 hits were the most since Bill Terry had 254 back in 1930. Carew's life-time batting mark jumped seven points to .335, a mark that ranks 26th on the all-time list. He outhit all other 1977 hitters by 50 points. National League champ Dave Parker of Pittsburgh was second at .338, the widest margin in baseball history.

He also won the American League's Most Valuable Player award for 1977. A player on a losing team almost never wins it.

In 1978 Carew again had the highest batting average in the American League. He hit .333 to lead the league in batting average for the fourth time. He also became the first player in an All-Star game to hit two triples in a single game. His seven league batting titles are surpassed only by Ty Cobb (12) and

Honus Wagner (8).

No, he hasn't hit .400 yet. But after 1977, almost everyone agrees that if anyone ever does it, it will be Rod Carew. "Of all the guys in the game right now, I think he can do it," said Williams, the man who knows more about hitting .400 than any man alive.

Or consider the opinion of Minnesota Manager Gene Mauch. "He is just amazing," said Mauch. "He has a long swing, yet he hits the ball all the time. I believe he would hit .400 in the National League with all of its artificial surfaces. Heck, he may hit .400 in this league."

The odds may not very good, but there are very few people betting against him.

Carl Yastrzemski

When Carl Yastrzemski retires from baseball, he will likely have 3,000 hits, a rare batting Triple Crown, three American League batting championships, a home run title and a runs batted in title.

But Yaz, as he has come to be known around the nation, will have more than all of that. 1967 will be remembered as his year, the "Year of Yastrzemski". It is an honor given to few men. Only rarely does one person dominate an entire sports season. But Yaz WAS baseball in 1967.

Carl Yastrzemski was born on August 22, 1939. He is the son of a Polish potato farmer in Southampton, Long Island,

New York. He was a good enough sandlot baseball player to attract many scouts. He turned down their offers and enrolled at Notre Dame.

He never played baseball there. Several teams bid on his services. He finally signed with Boston for a $100,000 bonus. Why the Red Sox?

"Father Joe, a family friend, pointed out two things about them," Yaz recalled later. "He considered them the lousiest team in baseball and said they had the greatest owner in baseball (Tom Yawkey). I felt like I'd have a good chance of making the team in a hurry and the money was right so I signed."

Yastrzemski had made a wise choice. Not long after his signing, the 19-year old shortstop was being labeled as the successor to Ted Williams. Yaz began his career in Raleigh in the Carolina League in 1959. He played both second base and shortstop. He led the league in hitting with a .377 batting mark. He also slammed 15 home runs and drove in 100 runs. He was the runaway choice as

Carolina League Player of the Year.

Up in the big leagues, Williams was getting old. The Red Sox' leftfielder was 42 years old. Although he had a batting average of over .300, he announced that he would retire at the end of 1960. The Boston management decided there was only one man who could fill Williams' place. The man was Yastrzemski.

Yaz was assigned to the Red Sox' Minneapolis farm club for 1960. There, he switched from the infield to the outfield without difficulty. At the same time he led the league in hits with 193 and batted .339. In 1961, he went to the majors to fill Williams' shoes.

The pressure on the 20-year old rookie outfielder was intense in the early going in 1961. His average reflected it. His average stuck around the .200 mark the first few months of the season. Yaz admitted later that he wasn't sure he would make it. But he finished the season strong. He ended with a .266 average, 11 home runs and 80 RBIs. Of the Red Sox starters, only Pete Runnels hit for a higher average. The Yastrzemski era had begun.

Yaz continued to improve at the plate and in the field during the next couple of seasons. But the Red Sox continued to lose. He won the American League batting title in 1963 with a .321 mark.

Unlike Williams, the new Boston star wasn't hitting many home runs. And the Red Sox continued to lose. He was named captain of the team. After winning the batting title in 1963, Carl's average dipped to .289 in 1964. His 15 home runs and 67 RBIs weren't close to being in the Williams' category. Of course, it wasn't a fair comparison. Very few players records compare to Williams' marks.

Yastrzemski's average bobbed back up above .300 in 1965 (.312), and his home run (20) and RBI (72) totals also jumped. But he was back down to .278 with 16 homers and 80 RBIs in 1966. Yaz was a Gold Glove outfielder and a good hitter. But Red Sox fans were still a little disappointed in Williams' successor. Until 1967, that is. That was the year when Boston fans stopped longing for the good old days.

When spring training began, there was really no reason to believe the season would be any different than the others. There was a new manager, Dick Williams. The club, however, was basically the same one that had finished ninth in the 10-team American League the year before.

The oddsmakers gave the Red Sox a 100-1 shot at winning the AL title. Even the new manager would only predict, "We'll win more than we lose."

But that was before anyone dreamed of the kind of season it would be for Yastrzemski. Minnesota, Chicago and Detroit were the league favorites. As August approached, the surprising Red Sox were bunched closely with those three teams. Yaz, meanwhile, was hitting more homers than he had ever hit. His batting mark was well above the .300 mark. He was making great plays in the outfield. He was the clearcut leader of the club.

At the end of August, Yaz went into a long slump. He was 0 for 18. Williams put him on the bench. On August 30, in the eighth inning of a 1-1 game against New York, Williams went to his best hitter one more time. In the 11th inning, Yaz did it. He slammed a homer that gave the Red Sox a 2-1 victory. He kept them in the pennant race.

Five days later, Williams again told the tired Yaz to take a rest. This time Yaz insisted on playing. He slugged two home runs and a single and drove in four runs. The Sox won again. It was the beginning of an unbelievable Yastrzemski show during the final two weeks of the season.

The White Sox dropped out of the race. The three remaining teams were running a close race as the season entered the final two days of play. Minnesota (91-69), Detroit (89-69) and Boston (90-70) all had a shot at the AL flag. It all depended on what they did the last two days. For the Red Sox to have a chance, they had to win both games. The Red Sox would be playing Minnesota. The Tigers had a chance to win their games and win it on their own.

Yaz, who had a chance to win the AL Triple Crown too, took care of the Boston part. In the next to last game of the season, the Twins struck first. The Sox bounced back with a run in the third to tie the game at 1-1. Yaz then singled in another run to make it 2-1 Boston. The two clubs swapped runs in the sixth to keep the Red Sox on top 3-2.

In the bottom of the seventh Yastrzemski hit the decider. The Red Sox got their first two runners on base. Twins' Manager Carl Ermer put left-handed Jim Merritt to face the left-swinging Yastrzemski. It was a waste of time. Yaz slammed one of Merritt's pitches into the Fenway Park bullpen. The Red Sox had a 6-2 lead and the game. It was Yastrzemski's 44th homer of the year. It gave him a one homer lead over the Twins' Harmon Killebrew. But Killebrew slugged one that day too. The Triple Crown bid, and the pennant, would come down to the final day.

In the final game Minnesota again scored first with single runs in the first and third. But Boston came back with five runs in the sixth. Two runs were driven in on a clutch single by Yaz. The Red Sox won it 5-3. The Tigers lost the second game of a double-header to California. The Red Sox had their first pennant in 21 years.

More than anyone else, Yastrzemski was responsible. He had gone seven for eight in the final two days. He had six RBIs. He was four for four on that last day. He didn't hit a last day homer, but neither did Killebrew. That was enough to give Yaz the AL batting title (.326), RBI title (126) and home run championship (44), a rare Triple Crown.

For the final two weeks of the season, the new superstar had hit an astounding .523. He followed up by hitting .400 in the seven-game World Series with the St. Louis Cardinals. Even so the Red Sox lost. At the end of the season he received every vote for the American League's Most Valuable Player Award but one.

He didn't just wilt and go away either. He led the AL in hitting again in 1968. He slugged 40 homers in both 1969 and 1970. His totals dropped sharply after that, but he remained a terror in the clutch. In 1972 he led a Red Sox stretch drive that just fell short.

The Red Sox began to find new stars like hard-hitting outfielders Jim Rice and Fred Lynn. But Yaz kept right on doing his job each year. In 1976 his batting average was only .267. But he had 21 homers and 102 RBIs. Boston finished third beyond the Yankees. Yaz was the Sox's Most Valuable Player.

In 1978, the 38-year old Yaz was still the reason that the talented Rice couldn't break into the regular outfield. Rice was used mostly as the designated hitter. The ageless Yaz was still simply too good. He would have again played on the American League All-Star team except for a sore back. He socked four home runs on four consecutive nights during the month of July. As the captain of the Red Sox, Yaz homered in the American League East championship game against the Yankees. That gave Boston the lead. Unfortunately, Boston lost the game 5-4.

He is still a fine hitter, although he has as much as admitted that his fielding skills are the key to how long he will play.

As the 1978 season wound down, Yaz had less than 20 hits to go to reach the 3,000 mark. If Yaz gets 3,000 hits, he will be only the 14th player to do it. Pete Rose became the 13th player to pass the 3,000-hit mark in 1978. "Sure, I'd like to get 3,000 hits," said Yaz. "But not if I have to embarrass myself to do it. When I can't play defense, I'll quit. No designated hitter for me."

Ted Williams probably wouldn't have done it either.